Read & Re...

FOR
KS1

PAGE
1

Read & Respond

FOR KS1

Author: Sylvia Clements

Development Editor: Rachel Mackinnon

Editor: Sarah Sodhi

Assistant Editor: Suzanne Adams

Series Designer: Anna Oliwa

Designer: Liz Gilbert

Illustrations: David Armitage and Shelagh McNicolas

Text © 2009, Sylvia Clements   © 2009 Scholastic Ltd

Designed using Adobe InDesign

Published by Scholastic Ltd, Villiers House,
Clarendon Avenue, Leamington Spa,
Warwickshire CV32 5PR
www.scholastic.co.uk
Printed by Bell & Bain
1 2 3 4 5 6 7 8 9   9 0 1 2 3 4 5 6 7 8

British Library Cataloguing-in-Publication Data
A catalogue record for this book is available from the British
Library.
ISBN 978-1407-11396-8

The right of Sylvia Clements to be identified as the author of this
work has been asserted by her in accordance with the Copyright,
Designs and Patents Act 1988.

Extracts from Primary National Strategy's Primary Framework
for Literacy (2006) http://nationalstrategies.standards.dcsf.
gov.uk/primary/primaryframework/ © Crown copyright.
Reproduced under the terms of the Click Use Licence.

All rights reserved. This book is sold subject to the condition
that it shall not, by way of trade or otherwise, be lent, hired out or
otherwise circulated without the publisher's prior consent in any
form of binding or cover other than that in which it is published
and without a similar condition, including this condition, being
imposed upon the subsequent purchaser.

No part of this publication may be reproduced, stored in a
retrieval system, or transmitted, in any form or by any means,
electronic, mechanical, photocopying, recording or otherwise,
without the prior permission of the publisher. This book remains
copyright, although permission is granted to copy pages where
indicated for classroom distribution and use only in the school
which has purchased the book, or by the teacher who has
purchased the book, and in accordance with the CLA licensing
agreement. Photocopying permission is given only for purchasers
and not for borrowers of books from any lending service.

Due to the nature of the web, we cannot guarantee the content
or links of any site mentioned. We strongly recommend that
teachers check websites before using them in the classroom.

Acknowledgements
The publishers gratefully acknowledge permission to reproduce
the following copyright material: **Scholastic Children's Books**
for the use of *The Lighthouse Keeper's Lunch* by Ronda and David
Armitage © 1977, Ronda and David Armitage (1977, Scholastic
Children's Books). Every effort has been made to trace copyright
holders for the works reproduced in this book, and the publishers
apologise for any inadvertent omissions.

The Lighthouse Keeper's Lunch

About the book

The Lighthouse Keeper's Lunch, first published over 30 years ago in 1977, has become a modern-day children's classic picture book. Every day, Mr Grinling, the lighthouse keeper, clambers down the steep, rocky cliffs and rows across the choppy sea to his lighthouse to clean and polish his light and make sure it shines brightly at night. At lunchtime he munches on his delicious lunch, lovingly and thoughtfully prepared by his wife, who sends the lunch in a basket, down a wire to the lighthouse. Mr Grinling, however, is not the only one who looks forward to the tasty food. Greedy seagulls intercept the perfect picnics on their journey down the wire. Mrs Grinling has to think of a way to stop the greedy seagulls from stealing the lighthouse keeper's lunch.

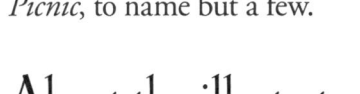

Aside from the tasty ingredients in Mrs Grinling's picnic basket, the story contains the ingredients for a superb cocktail of cross-curricular opportunities (as well as its obvious literacy links). It is an ideal stimulus for at least a half-term's creative curriculum scheme of work: the history of lighthouses; the story of Grace Darling; geographical locations of lighthouses around the British Isles; planning healthy eating in PSHE; design and technology ideas for solving Mr Grinling's lunch problem and designing healthy meals; science opportunities with circuits; art opportunities with seascapes; maths data collection and presentation; drama and home-corner role play; as well as endless opportunities for learning in ICT.

The story has a classically simple structure: a distinct beginning (where we are introduced to the setting and the main characters); a clearly identifiable middle (where the plot takes place in a sequenced series of events, using the days of the week to separate each event); and a pleasing ending that brings the story neatly to a close. This makes this book an ideal example for teaching story structure.

About the author

Ronda Armitage was born in New Zealand. She was a primary school teacher for a number of years and also trained as a counsellor, working in family therapy. She has written many children's books, the majority of which are illustrated by her husband, David, who is an artist. As well as children's fiction, she writes non-fiction family therapy books. Ronda has written a number of other books featuring Mr and Mrs Grinling and their marmalade cat, Hamish. These include *The Lighthouse Keeper's Catastrophe*, *The Lighthouse Keeper's Cat*, *The Lighthouse Keeper's Christmas* and *The Lighthouse Keeper's Picnic*, to name but a few.

About the illustrator

David Armitage has been an exhibitions officer for a city gallery and an art editor. His working life is divided between illustration, graphic design and painting. His artwork is exhibited in this country and abroad. *The Lighthouse Keeper's Lunch* was inspired by a visit with the children to Beachy Head. Since then Ronda and David have jointly published many picture books. David has also illustrated stories for other authors and written his own books.

Facts and figures
The Lighthouse Keeper's Lunch
Author: Ronda Armitage
Illustrator: David Armitage
First published: 1977 by Andre Deutsch Ltd.
It was Ronda Armitage's first book, and won the 1978 Esther Glen Award (New Zealand).
The Lighthouse Keeper's Lunch has been adapted for the stage by The Pied Piper Theatre Company, who specialise in presenting adaptations of well-known children's stories.

Guided reading

From cover to cover

Begin by showing the front cover of the book. Discuss the title and the authors. Why do the children think there are two names on the cover? Establish that it is a picture book and one is the author and one is the illustrator. Discuss the picture. Ask: *What is a lighthouse? Where would you find one? What do you think a lighthouse keeper does? Can you think of any other jobs that include the word keeper in the title?* (Zookeeper.) Discuss why the children think there is a rope with a basket attached to it going to the lighthouse. Can they deduce who may be sending it and what it will contain? Can they predict why the man on the cover looks rather grumpy?

Turn to the back cover and read the blurb. Ask: *What do we learn from the information given? Why is a question given without an answer?* Introduce the term *hook*. Discuss the other information and why it is included. Explain the term *review*. Have the children ever been influenced by a review of a film or a book? Discuss whether a bad review would be put on the back of a book. Ask: *Where might you be able to go to read a balanced viewpoint?* (On a book review website.)

Meet the Grinlings

Read the first four double-page spreads, ending *...on the rocks*. Explain that these pages are the introduction to the story. We immediately find out who the main characters are and where the story is set. We also find out a little about what the characters are like. Draw three spidergrams: one for each character and one for the setting. Invite the children to give you information about Mr Grinling and Mrs Grinling. Revisit the text, demonstrating how to locate information in the text and then inviting the children to tell you how to record the information on the spidergram. Discuss the meaning of *industrious*. Keep a permanent log of new vocabulary as there are quite a few new, ambitious words in the story.

Look at the picture of Mr Grinling sleeping and ask the children: *Why do you think he is smiling in his sleep?* (He knows that because he has worked so hard, the ships will be safe so he is contented.) *Why do you think the cat is smiling too?* (He is content to be sleeping on a soft, warm bed – typical cat behaviour.)

Look at the illustration of Mrs Grinling cooking. She is smiling. Ask: *What do you think she is thinking while she is busily cooking Peach Surprise?*

All at sea...

Discuss the setting. As the children describe the features of the setting, create a picture on the whiteboard. Discuss the fact that the cottage is on the mainland and the lighthouse is out at sea. Can the children explain how Mr Grinling travels to the lighthouse? (He has to climb down the cliff, down steep windy steps and row across by boat.) Why does Mr Grinling not simply take his lunch with him in the morning? (He has such a wonderful packed lunch it takes a whole morning to prepare.) After they have met the main characters and know the setting, ask the children to predict what is going to happen in the story. Look at the picture of Mrs Grinling sending the basket down the wire.

Monday ~ luscious lunch

Read the next double-page spread, ending *...down the wire*. Discuss the food that Mrs Grinling has prepared. Invite the children to select their favourite. Discuss the meaning of the word *appetising* and add it to the vocabulary log. Can the children find the words that describe the foods? (*Mixed, lighthouse, peach, iced, cold, assorted*.) Discuss what these words tell you about the food. Can the children suggest any further adjectives to make the foods sound even tastier?

Before continuing, ask the children to suggest what is going to happen. Then read the next two double-page spreads, from *But the lunch...* to *They'll have to try harder than this to stop us,*

Guided reading

Bert. Encourage the children to recount what happened in their own words. Using the context, establish the meaning of *scavenging, devoured, varmints, gusto* and *baffle.* Can the children tell how the story plot will progress? Does anyone guess the pattern of a new plan being hatched on each day until the Grinlings solve the problem?

Tuesday ~ must try harder

Look at the illustration of the seagulls untying the napkin. Has Mrs Grinling's plan worked? Read the next double-page spread, starting *On Tuesday evening...* and ending *"I'll have a tasty piece of herring waiting for you when you arrive home".* Compare the seagulls' speech bubbles and the Grinlings' direct speech. Challenge more confident readers to take on the role of Mr and Mrs Grinling and demonstrate how to identify the words that are spoken. Mrs Grinling plans how to solve the problem. What does this tell you about the two characters? Record and discuss the new vocabulary (*racked, brazen, accomplished, ingenious, secured, consolingly, herring*).

Wednesday ~ a fearful feline and bold, barefaced birds

Read all of Wednesday's events, from *Sadly, flying did not agree with Hamish* up to *just wait and see.* Ask: *Which words demonstrate that Hamish is not happy being in the basket? How does the picture show he is unhappy? How do you think Hamish is feeling on Wednesday evening?* (In the pictures he looks embarrassed, sheepish, ashamed and disgraced.) Once again, Mr Grinling asks Mrs Grinling to make the plan. What does this say about their characters? Invite three children to take on the parts of the birds. Encourage them to use expression. What sort of tone do they think they should use? Why? (A mocking tone as the birds are teasing and bullying Hamish, whereas usually the cat would be teasing them as this is the nature of cats. This is a good opportunity to discuss predators and

prey. Have the children ever seen a cat taunting a mouse or bird?)

Thursday and Friday ~ mean mustard mixtures

Before revealing Mrs Grinling's plan, ask the children to suggest what she could possibly think of to stop the naughty seagulls. Reveal the enormous mustard sandwich. Ask: *Have you ever eaten mustard? What did it taste like? Who normally eats it and with what? Why do you think Mr Grinling chuckled? Why was this a superb plan?* Discuss how the seagulls are always expecting something delicious but will be in for a nasty shock. Look at the birds' reactions. Talk about how sometimes one word says far more than a whole sentence. Ask: *What do the seagulls' reactions tell the reader? Why does Mrs Grinling repeat the mixture on Friday? What impact does this have?* Discuss what this tells you about the seagulls. Invite the children to consider what Mr Grinling did about his lunch on Thursday and Friday.

Saturday ~ jubilations!

Read to the end of the book, from *So, on Saturday...* Ask: *Which word describes how Mrs Grinling was feeling, now that her plan had worked?* Can the children think of any other words that would describe how pleased she was? We know that Mr Grinling is happy now. Can the children explain what he did that showed he was happy? (He sang sea shanties. Briefly explain what these are.) Once more, discuss the meaning of new vocabulary and reinforce how useful reading is for learning new words. Ask: *What did Mr Grinling see through his telescope? How will the fisherman react?* At the end Mr Grinling says, *"Ah well, such is life,"* before settling down to his amazing lunch. What do the children think he meant by this? Discuss the neat structure of the story and how the author used the days of the week to sequence the plot.

Guided reading

What a week!

After reading the whole book, use the story to encourage the children to recount the sequence of events through clearly directed questions: *What happened at the beginning of the week? On which day was this? What happened the next day? The problem was resolved by Saturday, what happened between Tuesday and Saturday?* Explain that the days of the week were used in the story to tell us when actions took place but that other words in the story were also used to tell us when events happened. Ask the children to be detectives and see if they can recall when the following time words were used in the story and what they told us: *Once…*, *at night time*, *sometimes*, *each morning*, *that evening*, *while*. Allow the children to use the text to scan for the examples. Write the sentences where each word was used on the board and use it to model another example. For example, text: *Sometimes at night, as Mr Grinling lay sleeping in his warm bed, the ships would toot.* Model: *Sometimes in the morning, as Mrs Grinling was cooking in her little kitchen, she would hum a cheerful song.*

Shared reading

Extract 1

● Discuss the story ingredients: characters, plot and setting. Recall the characters and settings of familiar stories.

● Sometimes settings determine the story plot, such as in 'The Three Billy Goats Gruff'. Can the children suggest and explain other examples?

● Read the extract on photocopiable page 8 without displaying the image. Ask: *Where does Mr Grinling live? What does* perched *mean? Where does he go every day? How do you think Mr Grinling gets to his boat? What does this tell you about the cottage in relation to the lighthouse?*

● Invite the children to explain why the setting will be important to the plot of this story.

● Ask: *What do we learn about Mr Grinling? What is his daily routine? What do you think* industrious *means? What does* tended *mean?* Give examples of other jobs where people have to tend to things, such as a shepherd who tends his sheep. Ask: *Why was it important for Mr Grinling to tend to his light all year round?*

Extract 2

● Before the plot commences, we meet the supporting main character, Mrs Grinling. Ask the children what Mrs Grinling did while Mr Grinling was polishing his light.

● This is a useful opportunity to introduce the advanced connective *while*. Choose two children and give them a mime to perform, such as brushing teeth and putting on shoes. Invite the class to create a sentence using *while*, such as *While Amy brushed her teeth, Mika put on his shoes*. Model writing the sentence.

● Study the illustration and ask the children to create a sentence using *while* for the images they see. For example, *While the basket travelled along the wire, the seagulls circled overhead*.

● What do the children think *concocting* means? What would they concoct for their own delicious lunch? In pairs, ask the children to imagine a delicious lunch and prepare to report back. Encourage them to use adjectives to enhance their descriptions, such as *juicy, crunchy, soft, fresh, spicy, sweet, succulent* and so on.

Extract 3

● This extract contains lots of advanced punctuation. First set the scene by asking: *What has happened in the day time? Where are the couple now? What are they talking about? What does* racked their brains *mean?* Establish that the seagulls have once again stolen the lunch and the couple are back in the little white cottage trying to work out what to do to solve the dilemma.

● Display an enlarged image of the couple talking to each other. Cut out two pairs of speech bubbles. Ask: *Which words would go in the speech bubbles? Which words would not be needed?* (*Said* and *exclaimed*.) Write the words spoken using one colour for Mr Grinling and a second colour for Mrs Grinling. Stick the bubbles to the picture.

● Ask what is special about the sentences spoken by Mr Grinling? (They are both questions and require question marks.)

● Can the children explain why Mrs Grinling's words have an exclamation mark? (She suddenly has a brainwave.) Can they predict what Mrs Grinling is going to do?

Extract 1

Once there was a lighthouse keeper called Mr Grinling. At night time he lived in a small white cottage perched high on the cliffs. In the day time he rowed out to his lighthouse on the rocks to clean and polish the light.

Mr Grinling was a most industrious lighthouse keeper. Come rain…

…or shine, he tended his light.

Text © 1977, Ronda Armitage; illustration © 1977, David Armitage.

Extract 2

Each morning while Mr Grinling polished the light Mrs Grinling worked in the kitchen of the little white cottage on the cliffs concocting a delicious lunch for him.

Once she had prepared the lunch she packed it into a special basket and clipped it onto a wire that ran from the little white cottage to the lighthouse on the rocks.

Text © 1977, Ronda Armitage; illustration © 1977, David Armitage.

PHOTOCOPIABLE

SECTION
3

Extract 3

On Wednesday evening Mr and Mrs Grinling racked their brains again for a new plan. "What shall we do?" said Mr Grinling.

Mrs Grinling looked thoughtful. "I have it!" she exclaimed. "Just the mixture for hungry seagulls."

"Indeed, my dear," said Mr Grinling. "What have you in mind?"

"Wait and see," said Mrs Grinling, "just wait and see."

Text © 1977, Ronda Armitage; illustration © 1977, David Armitage.

Plot, character and setting

A story sandwich

> **Objective:** To recognise the main elements that shape different texts.
> **What you need:** Copies of *The Lighthouse Keeper's Lunch*, photocopiable page 15, writing and drawing materials, soft toy cat (optional).
> **Cross-curricular link:** Art and design.

What to do

● Explain that stories are like sandwiches. The beginning and end are the two slices of bread and the centre is the filling – the exciting middle part where all the action takes place. Without the bread, the sandwich would fall apart, so we have to have a clear beginning and ending to make the story work. The more exciting the main events are, the tastier the sandwich will be.

● Invite the children to describe the beginning of the story and identify the pages in the book that constitute this part. Talk about what we learn from the introduction.

● Summarise the middle of the story together.

● Finally, identify the ending and discuss how it brings the story to a neat conclusion.

● Encourage the children to clearly distinguish each stage of the narrative by identifying what triggers the start of each section. Ask: *Which words signal the middle?* (*But one Monday…*) *Which words signal the ending?* (*So, on Saturday, up in the little white cottage on the cliffs…*)

● Use the photocopiable sheet to demonstrate understanding of the features of the narrative.

> **Differentiation**
> **For older/more confident learners:** Challenge children to complete the photocopiable sheet independently, writing sentences or putting key words in the boxes.
> **For younger/less confident learners:** Let children retell the story in a group with adult support, stopping to illustrate each box in the sandwich at relevant points.

Picturing the panorama

> **Objective:** To make adventurous word and language choices appropriate to the style and purpose of the text.
> **What you need:** Photocopiable page 16, Extract 1 on page 8, writing materials, whiteboards.
> **Cross-curricular links:** Art and design, ICT.

What to do

● Create a large collage of the setting for a class display, using a variety of appropriately coloured materials as the background.

● Use Extract 1 to identify the words that are used to describe the setting: *white, small.*

● Model how to annotate the photocopiable sheet with these two adjectives. Explain that the author has not used any adjectives to describe the cliffs, the sea, the wire, the boat or the lighthouse.

● Work as a class to think of adventurous describing words for one of the other setting features. For example, the cliffs may be described as: *rocky, craggy, steep* or *rugged.*

● Carry out the same activity for the remaining features in pairs (sea, wire, boat and lighthouse). Use whiteboards to practise blending and segmenting the chosen words to aid spelling.

> **Differentiation**
> **For older/more confident learners:** With a response partner, ask the children to write phrases or sentences to describe the setting features. For example, *The craggy cliffs dropped steeply down to the swirling water below.*
> **For younger/less confident learners:** In shared writing let children contribute their own language choices to an adult. The adult will encourage the group to make inventive and creative choices to extend their vocabulary.

Plot, character and setting

Through the telescope

> **Objective:** To make adventurous word and language choices appropriate to the style and purpose of the text.
> **What you need:** Cardboard tubes, coloured paper, Cellophane, sticky tape, writing materials.
> **Cross-curricular links:** Art and design, science.

What to do

● Return to the end of the story where Mr Grinling is surveying the coastline through his telescope. The picture shows us what Mr Grinling sees, but there is no text to describe his view. Use guided writing on the class whiteboard to model a description of what he sees. For example, *a small wooden fishing boat, a large wicker picnic basket, a fisherman in a checked jacket and three cheeky seagulls.* Model the use of capital letters and full stops.
● Invite the children to make their own telescopes using card tubes with a Cellophane end for the lens. Use this opportunity to explain how the lens brings objects closer. Also use magnifying glasses and microscopes to make close observations of objects.
● Using any of the viewing tools, encourage the children to write a description of their observations. Ensure they only focus on one particular view and stick with it.

> **Differentiation**
> **For older/more confident learners:** In pairs, ask the children to describe what they can see to their partner. Support children in extending their sentences to include extra information. For example, *I can see the beanbag* can become *I can see the spotty, cotton beanbag,* through prompting with questions. Encourage peers to ask questions to increase the information being given.
> **For younger/less confident learners:** Provide a sentence starter to support the children's writing as they describe what they can see through their telescope. For example, *Through my telescope, I can see…*

Mr and Mrs Grinling

> **Objective:** To identify the main characters in stories, and find specific information in simple texts.
> **What you need:** Copies of *The Lighthouse Keeper's Lunch*, photocopiable page 17, writing materials, word-processing package, computers.
> **Cross-curricular links:** Art and design, ICT.

What to do

● Explain that we learn about a character from what they do, what they say and how they look. Draw a three-column table on the board with the headings: Do, Say and Look.
● Begin with how Mr Grinling looks. Record the children's ideas from the pictures and use the opportunity to introduce and explain new vocabulary, such as *stocky, balding* and *cheery.*
● Move on to find evidence of Mr Grinling's actions that show what he is like (*hard-working, reliable* and *conscientious*).
● Finally, ask the children to identify some of the things he says that demonstrate his character. For example, *"A truly superb plan my dear, truly superb".* This shows how agreeable and approving Mr Grinling is towards his wife's ideas.
● Encourage the use of ICT skills to create a speech bubble of the words he says that best illustrate his personality.
● Carry out the same activity for Mrs Grinling using the photocopiable sheet.

> **Differentiation**
> **For older/more confident learners:** Children write sentences independently to describe Mrs Grinling and illustrate them with a drawing. Encourage them to use the text to find evidence and quotes.
> **For younger/less confident learners:** In a supported group, collate words to describe what Mrs Grinling says, does and looks like. Refer to specific parts of the text and use questions to prompt a response. Use ICT skills to create word cards and a speech bubble to display around the collage.

Plot, character and setting

SECTION

4

Fred, Tom and Bert

> **Objectives:** To visualise and comment on events, characters and ideas, making imaginative links to their own experiences; to explain their reactions to texts, commenting on important aspects.
> **What you need:** Copies of *The Lighthouse Keeper's Lunch*, whiteboards and writing materials, computers, word-processing package.
> **Cross-curricular links:** Art and design, ICT.

What to do
● Discuss all the things the seagulls did in the story. Invite the children to explain what impact this had on the plot.
● Show the pages that feature the seagulls. Prompt discussion by asking: *What do they do?* (They spot the lunch basket and help themselves to the picnic; they untie the napkin and steal the food; they taunt and tease Hamish; they are taken by surprise when they munch on the mustard; and eventually they fly off elsewhere to scavenge someone else's lunch.)

● Ask what each action tells you about their personalities. (They are greedy, mischievous and cheeky.) Discuss the children's experiences when they have behaved in a certain way, and what their actions say about them.
● Invite the children to make seagulls for a display, using paint or collage to decorate them. Let the children write words or sentences to describe the seagulls following on from the discussions. Surround the seagulls with the children's words and sentences.

> **Differentiation**
> **For older/more confident learners:** Provide a sentence skeleton for the children to use to describe the seagulls. For example, *The seagulls were... because they...* They can use this structure to write their own independent sentences.
> **For younger/less confident learners:** Let the children word process adjectives that describe the seagulls and display them around the seagull collages.

Plot plotting!

> **Objective:** To identify the main events and characters in stories, and find specific information in simple texts.
> **What you need:** Copies of *The Lighthouse Keeper's Lunch*, art materials, whiteboards, two coloured whiteboard pens for each group, computers, word-processing package.
> **Cross-curricular links:** Art and design, ICT.

What to do
● Recap the events of the middle of the story. Explain that the days of the week are used to help the reader see the progression of events.
● Put the children in six groups. Allocate one day to each group and provide a copy of the relevant pages. Ask the groups to discuss what happened and draft a recount of the events, beginning with a time connective, such as *On Monday...*

● Assist the children with their editing skills. Provide them with a different-coloured pen to tick or amend as appropriate in response to your questions: *Have you got a capital letter? Have you got a full stop? Does the sentence make sense?*
● Make a basket for each group to hang on the display wire. Help them to word process their recounts and attach them to the baskets in order.

> **Differentiation**
> **For older/more confident learners:** Recounting Tuesday's and Wednesday's events requires a higher level of inference and there is far more detail for children to recount. They may state what happened and subordinate with *but*.
> **For younger/less confident learners:** Children work with an adult to read the event for their day (Thursday or Friday) and compose their sentence to recount the event in response to open questions.

PAGE

13

Plot, character and setting

When and why?

Objective: To write simple and compound sentences and begin to use subordination in relation to time and reason.
What you need: Copies of *The Lighthouse Keeper's Lunch*, photocopiable page 18, writing materials, large, bright question cards reading *When?* and *Why?*

What to do
● During shared writing, demonstrate how to use subordination for time to sequence and connect events. Illustrate how a simple sentence can be extended to give more information.
● To do this, provide a simple sentence that describes an event in the story. For example, *Mr Grinling polished his light.* Explain that we want to give the reader more information. Hold up the *When?* question card and ask: *When did Mr Grinling polish his light?* Responses may include *every day* or *come rain or shine.* Demonstrate how to incorporate this to form a more complex sentence: *Every day, Mr Grinling polished his light.*
● Ask for another example of an action and write it on the whiteboard. Show the *When?* card and pose the question. Incorporate the time phrase to subordinate the sentence.
● Let the children create their own sentences using appropriate levels of support.

Differentiation
For older/more confident learners: With adult support, extend the sentence further to explain why. For example, *Why did Mr Grinling polish his light? Every day, Mr Grinling polished his light in order to stop the ships from crashing on the rocks.* Provide the children with a set of word cards of subordinating connectives, such as *so that* and *in order to.*
For younger/less confident learners: Let the children read the sentences on the photocopiable sheet before matching the correct time connective to the sentence, using the phrases provided.

When Saturday comes…

Objective: To draw on knowledge and experience of texts in deciding and planning what and how to write.
What you need: Writing materials.
Cross-curricular link: Design and technology.

What to do
● Recap what happened on Thursday and Friday and how these events led to the climax and ending of the story on the Saturday. Ask: *What happened on Sunday?* (Sunday is not mentioned.)
● Explain that the class is going to rewrite the story with a different ending. Invite the children to imagine that on Saturday, instead of looking elsewhere for food, one of the seagulls suggested trying for a third time (explain the saying *third time lucky*), knowing that Mrs Grinling was trying to outsmart them.
● What do the children think would happen on Saturday evening in the little white cottage? Ask them to talk with a partner, planning an idea for a seagull-proof method of transporting the lunch. Maybe Mr Grinling sets to work in his workshop building a wooden basket with a lockable lid?
● Use the text structure and knowledge of the characters to model how to write an extra section of text to describe what Mrs Grinling's final ingenious plan is. Finish with the successful delivery of the lunch on Sunday morning.

Differentiation
For older/more confident learners: Give the children the text for Wednesday evening and tell them to use it to model writing their own text for Saturday evening.
For younger/less confident learners: Model the text in response to a child's suggestions or give the children a simple cloze passage to structure the text and insert their own ideas.

A story sandwich

- Complete the story sandwich with drawings and words to show the ingredients that make up *The Lighthouse Keeper's Lunch*.

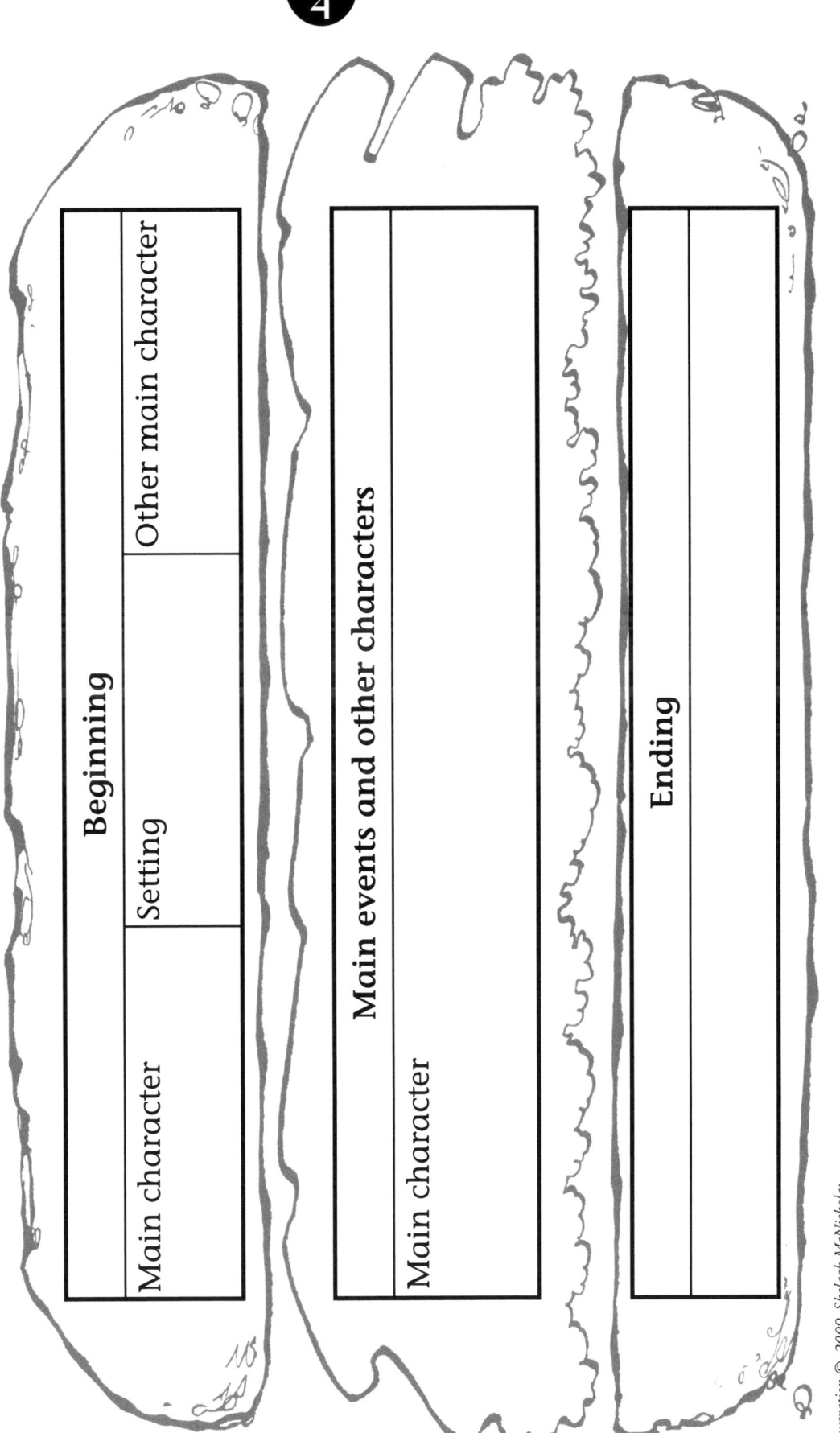

Beginning

Main character	Setting	Other main character

Main events and other characters

Main character

Ending

Illustration © 2009, Shelagh McNicholas.

Plot, character and setting

Picturing the panorama

- Work with your group or partner to carefully choose adventurous words to describe the setting.
- Make sure your words create a clear picture of the setting.
- Add your chosen adjectives to the scene in the boxes provided.

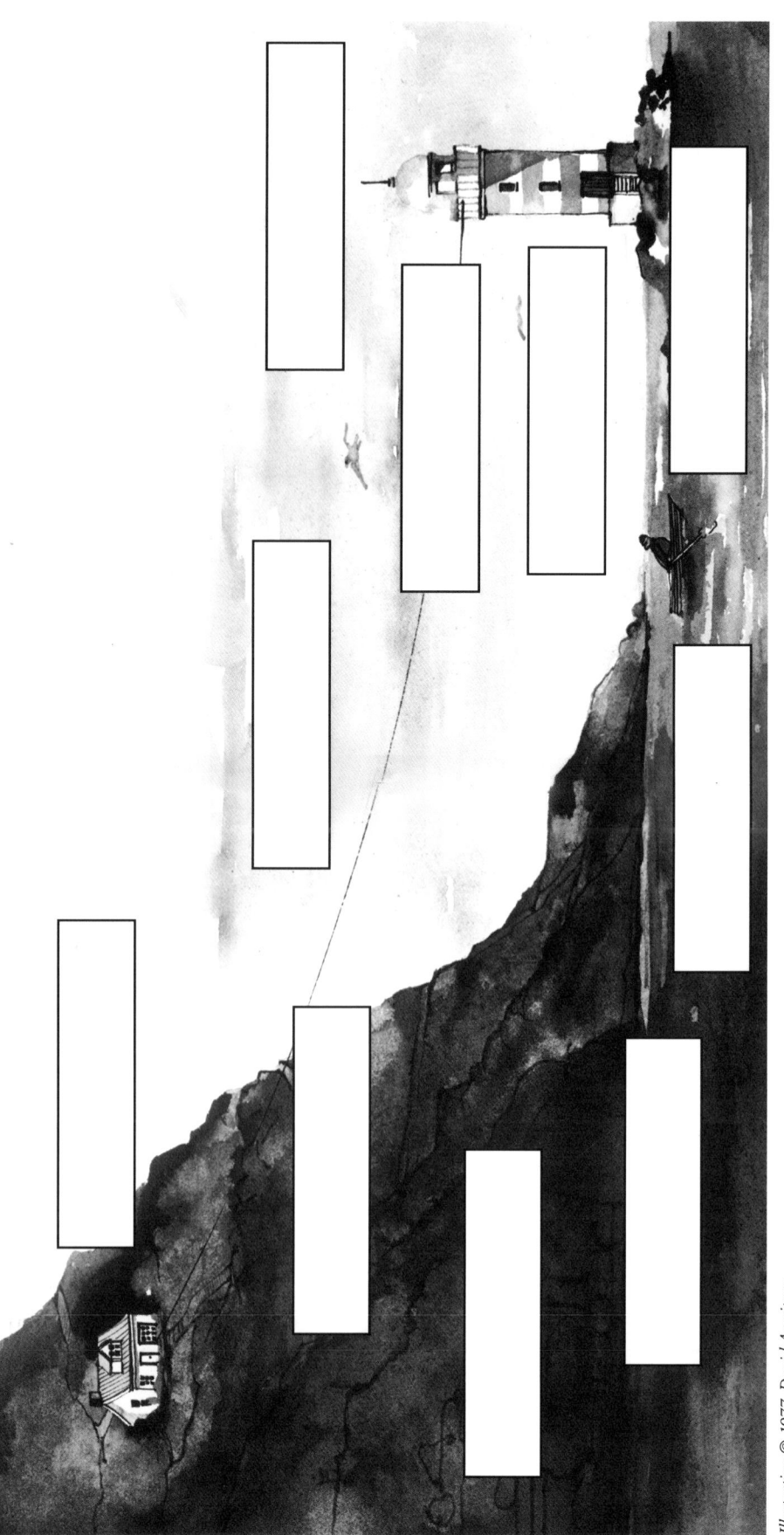

Illustration © 1977, David Armitage.

Mr and Mrs Grinling

We learn about a character from how they look, what they do and what they say.

● Write three words below the picture to describe how Mrs Grinling looks.

● Complete the sentences below with things that Mrs Grinling does that show what she is like. The first one has been done for you.

● Fill in the speech bubble with words that Mrs Grinling says. What does this tell you about her?

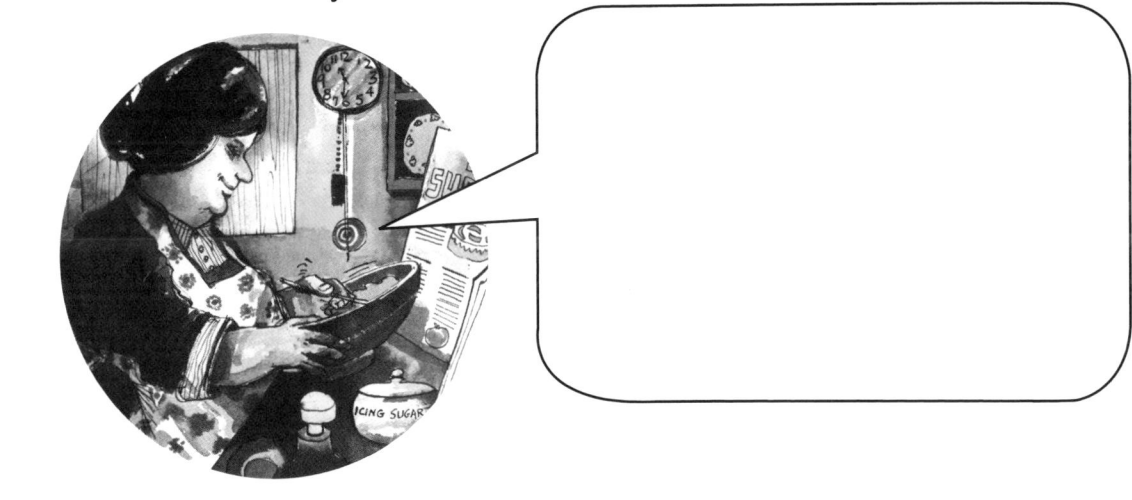

I think Mrs Grinling is **clever** because she **thinks of lots of ideas to try to stop the pesky seagulls**.

I think Mrs Grinling is _____ because she _____

_____.

I think Mrs Grinling is _____ because she _____

_____.

Illustration © 1977, David Armitage.

Plot, character and setting

When and why?

- Read each sentence. Then read the **when?** question. Next choose the correct time phrase from the box below.
- Write out your answers in full. The first one has been done for you.

1 Mr Grinling polished his light.
When did Mr Grinling polish his light?
Every day, Mr Grinling polished his light.

2 The ships tooted their horns.
When did the ships toot their horns?

_____

3 Mrs Grinling worked in the kitchen.
When did Mrs Grinling work in the kitchen?

_____

4 Mrs Grinling clipped the basket on a wire.
When did Mrs Grinling clip the basket on a wire?

_____

5 Mr And Mrs Grinling thought of a plan.
When did Mr And Mrs Grinling think of a plan?

_____

6 Mr Grinling sang sea shanties.
When did Mr Grinling sing sea shanties?

_____

Time phrases

Every day,   Sometimes at night,   Each morning,   That evening,
After packing the lunch,   While he waited for his lunch,

PHOTOCOPIABLE

SCHOLASTIC
www.scholastic.co.uk

READ & RESPOND: Activities based on *The Lighthouse Keeper's Lunch*

Talk about it

Hamish hand puppets

> **Objective:** To explore familiar themes and characters through improvisation and role play.
> **What you need:** Photocopiable page 22, felt, stick-on eyes, balls of wool, plastic needles, PVA glue, black felt-tipped pens, writing materials.
> **Cross-curricular link:** Art and design.

What to do

● Read the section where Hamish is placed in the basket, up to *On Wednesday evening…* Use the photocopiable sheet to create Hamish hand puppets to use for role play.
● In pairs, invite the children to each think of a question to ask Hamish about his experience. For example: *How did you feel when Mrs Grinling tried to put you in the basket? What was it like travelling in the basket? What could you see as you travelled along the wire? What scared you the most about your journey? How did you feel when the seagulls were teasing you?*
● Come together in a circle. Ask a volunteer to be Hamish and sit in Hamish's basket in the centre.
● Carry out the hot-seating activity, inviting pairs of children to ask Hamish their questions.
● Once the process has been demonstrated and the children feel secure with the role play, let them continue the activity in their groups.

> **Differentiation**
> **For older/more confident learners:** Let the children take on the role of Mr or Mrs Grinling and pose questions to Hamish in role.
> **For younger/less confident learners:** Encourage the children to play with their hand puppets and act out Hamish's journey. Follow this up by asking questions about what happened to Hamish and how he felt.

The Lighthouse Keeper's Lunch on stage

> **Objective:** To act out their own and well-known stories using voices for characters.
> **What you need:** Copies of *The Lighthouse Keeper's Lunch*, class whiteboard.

What to do

● Explain how a book is adapted for the screen or stage and detail the basic conventions of a playscript. Show the children examples, such as *The Jungle Book.*
● Using Monday's events, ask the children open questions to devise a script with speaking parts for Mrs Grinling (who may speak to Hamish), Mr Grinling and the seagulls. Record it on the class whiteboard.
● Model how to write the script including stage directions and a narrator. Invite the children to contribute and model how to form their ideas into sentences, highlighting the use of capital letters and full stops, and reading back to check that the sentence makes sense. Demonstrate how to edit the sentence, if it could be improved.
● Encourage the children to use the script to create their own mini performance.
● The story has been written as a musical version by David Wood, *The Lighthouse Keeper's Lunch: a musical play* (Josef Weinberger Ltd). The adaptation includes the libretto, the piano/vocal score and a CD with rehearsal accompaniment and performance accompaniment. If the book is being used for a whole scheme of work, this resource will be very useful.

> **Differentiation**
> **For older/more confident learners:** Working in a small group with adult support, invite the children to devise a simple playscript for a different part of the story.
> **For younger/less confident learners:** Let the children play-act parts of the story in the home corner using adult support for focusing and prompting.

Talk about it

When I packed Mr Grinling's lunch...

> **Objective:** To listen to others in class, ask relevant questions and follow instructions.
> **What you need:** Small wicker basket, pen, paper, photocopiable page 23 (laminated and cut up).

What to do

● Sit the class in a circle. Use a small basket to act as the signal for who is allowed to speak.
● Invite all the children to imagine they are Mrs Grinling. Explain that the aim of the activity is to listen and recall each item as it is added to the basket.
● The first person begins, *When I packed Mr Grinling's lunch, I put in the basket a...* The child must choose an item supported by an adjective, such as *a juicy peach* or *a spicy meatball.*

Use the word cards on the photocopiable sheet as prompts to introduce new vocabulary.
● The basket is passed on to the next person who recalls the previous item and adds a further item.
● Continue playing until everyone has had a turn. It is a good idea for an adult to make a note of the items. Encourage the children to listen and only contribute if they are directly asked, enabling quieter children to participate equally.

> **Differentiation**
> **For older/more confident learners:** Encourage the children to widen their vocabulary choices by introducing them to new, more ambitious synonyms for the adjectives chosen.
> **For younger/less confident learners:** Let the children simply suggest a food item without a description.

Little white cottage and the lighthouse home corner

> **Objective:** To explore familiar themes and characters through improvisation and role play.
> **What you need:** Role-play area, kitchen furniture and equipment, food, large cardboard box, paint, oars, CD player, sea shanties or songs on CD, two chairs, rope and basket pulley system, torch, aprons, handkerchief, hat, toy cat, basket, dusters, brushes.
> **Cross-curricular link:** Art and design.

What to do

● Develop a three-part lighthouse keeper's role-play area, to facilitate learning through play.
● In the first part, the cottage and Mrs Grinling's kitchen, include word labels on the food and equipment and simple recipe cards. Set up two chairs where Mr and Mrs Grinling can plan their strategies. This should link to the lighthouse with a pulley system.
● For the second part, invite the class to build a

boat with oars by painting a large cardboard box. Place a CD player in the boat with sea shanties or songs for children to sing along to.
● In the third area, the lighthouse, include a pretend light for tending to and a pulley system linked to the cottage. The pulley system can be used to send the basket between the two areas.
● The role-play area can be used to extend and enrich learning, as well as providing a valuable activity for a group to do while other groups are working on focused tasks. Use the opportunity to make recorded observations.

> **Differentiation**
> **For older/more confident learners:** Provide differentiated word cards in the kitchen area.
> **For younger/less confident learners:** Allow the children to role play freely. Observe to assess each child's progress and identify areas of talk, drama and group interaction that need moving forward.

Talk about it

Pulley power

Objective: To explain ideas and processes using imaginative and adventurous vocabulary and non-verbal gestures to support communication.
What you need: Copies of *The Lighthouse Keeper's Lunch*, string or rope, grooved wheels (pulley or block), basket, photocopiable page 24.
Cross-curricular links: Design and technology, science.

What to do

● Show the class the picture of Mrs Grinling sending the basket to the lighthouse.
● In the picture, the basket travels to the lighthouse due to the mass of the basket and gravity. Ask: *Have you ever been on a zip wire? Can you explain how it feels and what happens?*
● Invite the children to suggest how the basket is returned to the cottage, after looking carefully at the front cover. (Mr Grinling must take it in his boat.) Recreate the system in the hall using rope, a pulley wheel, basket and gym equipment

to recreate the height difference. Pay attention to health and safety aspects. Can the children describe what they see? Does it travel at the same speed the whole way?
● Investigate how Mrs Grinling could use a pulley system to retrieve the basket. Discuss why this may be necessary. (In bad weather, Mr Grinling may have to stay overnight.)
● With adult support, allow the children to investigate creating pulley systems to pull the load back up to the cottage.
● Encourage the children to draw and annotate their pulley systems after the investigation.

Differentiation
For older/more confident learners: Invite the children to use the photocopiable sheet to record and explain their findings independently.
For younger/less confident learners: Give the children adult support and work as a group to draw and explain what they found.

Mr Grinling – is that you?

Objective: To take turns to speak, listen to others' suggestions and talk about what they are going to do.
What you need: Hall space, large sheets of paper, marker pens, paper cups, string, telephone ringtone.
Cross-curricular link: PSHE.

What to do

● Set the scene: It is Monday morning, about 11 o'clock. Mr Grinling has just received an empty picnic basket. He is going to telephone Mrs Grinling and tell her the bad news. Mrs Grinling will respond and describe all the lovely dishes she had prepared for him. They will express their feelings about the situation and discuss what they think has happened and what they will do.
● Sit in a circle in the hall and, using two large sheets of paper, one for Mr Grinling and one for Mrs Grinling, discuss how the events made the characters feel. Scribe how they would speak and

what they would say to express these feelings. Recall the lovely dishes Mrs Grinling had prepared and make up some more.
● Let the children work in pairs to pretend to be Mr and Mrs Grinling, with a string telephone.
● Circulate and listen to the conversations. Invite pairs who perform well to carry out their conversation in front of the class.
● Let the children swap partners and repeat the process.

Differentiation
For older/more confident learners: Challenge the children to record their conversations as a piece of written dialogue or a playscript.
For younger/less confident learners: Let the children take turns with an adult in the role of Mrs Grinling. The adult should lead the conversation, asking open questions and encouraging the children to respond appropriately.

Hamish hand puppets

You will need

- Orange felt
- Black felt
- Two stick-on eyes
- Wool or pipe-cleaners
- Glue
- Needle
- Thread
- Black felt-tipped pen

What to do

- Cut out the front and back body pieces in orange felt.
- Sew the two pieces together.
- Cut out two ears in orange felt and glue on to the body.
- Cut out a nose in black felt and glue into place.
- Stick on the two eyes.
- Draw on a smiley mouth in black felt-tipped pen.
- Stick on the wool or pipe-cleaners as whiskers.

Body

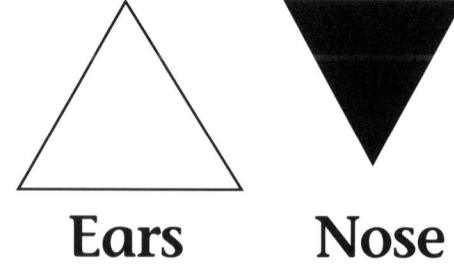

Ears   **Nose**

www.scholastic.co.uk

READ & RESPOND: Activities based on *The Lighthouse Keeper's Lunch*

When I packed Mr Grinling's lunch…

● Use these cards to play a matching game. Place the cards face down and, in pairs, take turns to reveal two cards. If they make a correct pair, the player keeps the pair. If not, turn them back over. The winner is the player with the most pairs.

crunchy	juicy	spicy	sickly
refreshing	savoury	crusty	sour

Illustration © 2009, Shelagh McNicholas.

SCHOLASTIC
www.scholastic.co.uk

PHOTOCOPIABLE

Pulley power

- Draw and label how Mr Grinling's lunch is delivered from the cottage to the lighthouse.

- Draw and label how the basket can be returned to the cottage along the wire using a pulley system.

Word bank

pulley	wire	gravity	push	pull	force
	rope	basket	hook		

Get writing

A week in the life of a lighthouse keeper

Objectives: To use planning to establish clear sections for writing; to use appropriate language to make sections hang together.
What you need: Copies of *The Lighthouse Keeper's Lunch*, whiteboards, pens, pencils, colouring pencils, paper.
Cross-curricular link: Art and design.

What to do
● Tell the children that they are going to write the events of *The Lighthouse Keeper's Lunch* from Monday to Saturday in their own words.
● Together, discuss what happened on each of the six days. Record key spellings on the board for use in independent writing.
● Ask the children to write one sentence for each day. Model writing the first sentence, demonstrating the use of connectives to extend sentences. For example, *On Monday, Mrs Grinling made a lovely lunch for Mr Grinling but it did not get to the lighthouse because the pesky seagulls stole the food.*
● Invite the children to write their sentences on individual whiteboards. Encourage them to check capital letters, full stops and whether their sentences make sense, and to underline of any spellings they think may be incorrect. Can the children identify and tick their connectives?
● Provide six pages, one for each day in their story, with writing lines and space for their illustrations. Collate the pages into a book and make a cover.

Differentiation
For older/more confident learners: Encourage the children to write their sentences independently, incorporate new, ambitious vocabulary and use dictionaries to assist them with their spelling.
For younger/less confident learners: Provide the sentences for each picture on cards for the children to order and copy.

Tom, Bert and Fred

Objective: To use capital letters and full stops when punctuating simple sentences.
What you need: Copies of *The Lighthouse Keeper's Lunch*, photocopiable page 28, writing materials.

What to do
● Discuss how dialogue is presented and demonstrate on the board. Explain that spoken words are enclosed in speech marks. Invite the children to suggest something one of the characters may have said. Use this to model how to write a piece of dialogue, focusing solely on the location of the speech marks.
● Ask how the words spoken by the seagulls were presented in the story (using speech bubbles). Discuss how speech marks and speech bubbles differ, and when and why they are used. Demonstrate how to transfer the words from one of the speech bubbles into a piece of dialogue using speech marks.
● Give the children the photocopiable sheet and ask them to identify the words spoken by the seagulls and write them into the speech bubbles. They should focus on identifying the correct words to include, and correctly using capital letters and full stops for each sentence.
● In the plenary session, invite the children to read out their spoken words in role.

Differentiation
For older/more confident learners: With adult support, let the children write the words spoken by the seagulls in the book as a piece of dialogue. Discuss how the words would have been spoken.
For younger/less confident learners: Assist the children by working with them to highlight the spoken words, before writing in the speech bubbles.

Get writing

What is a lighthouse?

> **Objective:** To write chronological and non-chronological information texts using simple structures.
> **What you need:** Access to lighthouse websites, information books, pictures of lighthouses, A3 paper.
> **Cross-curricular link:** Art and design.

What to do

● In preparation for this activity, paint a picture of a classic lighthouse on A3 paper as the front cover for a class information booklet about lighthouses. Produce a cut-out lighthouse page for each child, the same size as the cover and lined for writing. Invite everyone to contribute a page towards the class book about lighthouses.
● Discuss: *What are lighthouses? When were they first invented? Who invented them? Where are lighthouses found? Why are they located in these places? What are they used for? Who are they important to? Why are they so important? How are they operated?*
● Demonstrate how to mind-map ideas on a spidergram, by placing the overall topic in the centre (lighthouses) and using one branch for each category of information.
● Split into groups and allocate each group one research area. The research will be most effectively carried out with adult support. Carry out the research throughout the week, and complete the writing activity once all the necessary information has been gathered.

> **Differentiation**
> **For older/more confident learners:** Allocate the more complex areas of research to this group.
> **For younger/less confident learners:** Provide the information required to answer the group's question. Read the information together and then plan and draft sentences on whiteboards.

The story of Grace Darling

> **Objectives:** To write chronological and non-chronological information texts using simple structures; to draw on knowledge and experience of texts in deciding and planning what and how to write.
> **What you need:** Photocopiable page 29, writing materials, booklets.
> **Cross-curricular links:** ICT, art and design, history.

What to do

● Invite the children to explain what is meant by 'a famous person'. Can they name any famous people? Can they explain why these people are famous? Ask: *How do people become famous?* Encourage them to suggest people from the past and present and list the names and reasons for them being famous on the board.
● Introduce and tell the story of Grace Darling (the RNLI website www.rnli.org.uk contains an animated version).
● Ask open questions to gather information and vocabulary on the board to support independent writing: *Who was Grace Darling? Where did she live? What would it have been like living there? What job did Grace and her father do? What happened to the Forfarshire on 7 September 1838? What happened to the people? How do you think the people felt who managed to clamber on to the rocks? What did Grace do? How do you think she felt in the small boat in that terrible storm?*
● Let the children use the photocopiable sheet to retell the story of Grace Darling in their own words.

> **Differentiation**
> **For older/more confident learners:** Challenge the children to plan their own version of Grace Darling's story, to write up as an illustrated book with a cover.
> **For younger/less confident learners:** Working with support, let the children draft a sentence for each picture on their whiteboard before writing it on to the photocopiable sheet.

Get writing

Lighthouses around the UK

Objectives: To compose and write simple sentences independently to communicate meaning; to use capital letters and full stops when punctuating simple sentences; to compose sentences using tense consistently (present and past).
What you need: Photocopiable page 30, access to the internet, printer, large outline map of the UK, labels.
Cross-curricular links: ICT, geography.

What to do
● Show the children a map of the UK. Talk about the UK being an island. Discuss features of the coast and why lighthouses might be needed. Discuss compass points and identify North, South, East and West.
● Use the internet to show the children photographs of different lighthouses around the UK. Trinity House is the general lighthouse authority for England, Wales, The Channel Islands and Gibraltar. The website contains useful photographs and information.
● Record details about four or five lighthouses on the class whiteboard.
● Let the children use the photocopiable sheet to record facts and write simple, full sentences about one of the lighthouses. Use this writing exercise as an opportunity to discuss tense.
● Encourage the children to use ICT skills to locate and print a photograph of each lighthouse for display around a UK map alongside their work.

Differentiation
For older/more confident learners: Challenge the children to research extra information and write more detailed sentences about their lighthouse.
For younger/less confident learners: Provide cut-up, whole sentences for the children to arrange and write up.

What shall we put in Mr Grinling's basket?

Objective: To make adventurous word and language choices appropriate to the style and purpose of the text.
What you need: Whiteboard, recorded or live music and/or percussion instruments, recorders, sheet music for 'Drunken Sailor'.
Cross-curricular link: Music.

What to do
● Explain what a sea shanty is. 'Drunken Sailor' is one of the best-known and was first sung in the 1830s. It was the only type of work song permitted in the Navy and was known as a 'stamp'n'go' song. Play the traditional version and discuss the lyrics.
● Teach the children one or two verses to get a feel for the rhythm and pattern.
● Write a class version entitled 'What shall we put in Mr Grinling's basket?' Invite the children to give ideas for different foods. Collate verbs, such as *bake*, *spread*, *whisk* and *mix*, and a range of adjectives to describe the food.
● Model the first verse. For example, *Bake him a cake with chocolate icing* (repeat three times), *Early in the morning*. Use different colours for each part of speech. The children can then use this to provide a structure for their verse.
● Suggest that the chorus could refer to Mrs Grinling getting up early or to the basket being raised up and attached to the wire.
● Independently, children write their own verse.

Differentiation
For older/more confident learners: Challenge the children to write independently, being guided to find and try out more ambitious vocabulary.
For younger/less confident learners: Support the children to focus on the rhythm and syllable count of words.

Tom, Bert and Fred

● Read the sentences below.

● Write the words that are being spoken into the speech bubbles. Do not forget to use capital letters to start your sentences and full stops or question marks to end them.

"Look down there." cried Bert to his two friends.

"What can you see?" asked Tom, as he flew faster to catch up with his friend.

"It's a basket full of yummy food." shouted Fred, swooping down to have a closer look.

Illustration © 1977, David Armitage.

■SCHOLASTIC
www.scholastic.co.uk

Get writing

SECTION
6

The story of Grace Darling

● Use the pictures to retell the story of Grace Darling.

Illustration © 2009, Shelagh McNicholas.

SCHOLASTIC
www.scholastic.co.uk

PAGE
29

PHOTOCOPIABLE

READ & RESPOND: Activities based on *The Lighthouse Keeper's Lunch*

Lighthouses around the UK

- Complete the fact box below about your chosen lighthouse.
- Using the facts, write one sentence in each box around the lighthouse.
- Colour the lighthouse scene.

Fact box	
Name of lighthouse	
Location	
Date built	
Height	
Interesting fact	

Illustration © 2009, Shelagh McNicholas.

SCHOLASTIC
www.scholastic.co.uk

Assessment

Assessment advice

The learning objectives for all activities in this book have been derived from the 12 strands of learning identified in the Primary Framework. The objectives have been chosen from Years 1 and 2. However, the learning objectives need to be right for each child at each stage of their learning. Therefore, assessment of an individual's needs may require tracking back or forward through a progression strand in order to tailor objectives to individuals or groups of children. This in turn will allow the development of clear success criteria for each activity.

When using each activity, make sure there are clear child-friendly success criteria for each task and that the children fully understand what the success criteria are and what they need to do to meet them.

Using traffic-light systems for the children to complete to show how well they consider they have met their success criteria is one way of developing self-assessment. You can also use the traffic-light system for their own recording. Children can colour a box next to their success criteria to provide evidence of self-assessment. The meanings of the three colours are:

Red: I need lots more practice.

Amber: I am quite secure but need a bit more practice.

Green: I am confident.

It happened like this…

> **Assessment focus:** To use *The Lighthouse Keeper's Lunch* as a stimulus for independent writing, to provide a piece of evidence against assessment focuses in reading and writing, according to individual children's assessment needs.
>
> **What you need:** Photocopiable page 32, writing materials.

What to do
● Hand out the photocopiable sheet. Ask the children to imagine that the headteacher has asked to borrow *The Lighthouse Keeper's Lunch* to read, having admired all the children's lovely work, and is really excited to share the story. However, the book has been lost, so in order to avoid disappointing him or her, the children need to explain what the story was about using the character pictures as prompts.

● Let the children use the photocopiable sheet to write about the characters and the role they played in the story. Explain that the first sentence should describe who is shown in the picture. The second and subsequent sentences should describe something of relevance about the character and their role in the story. For example: *This is Mrs Grinling, the lighthouse keeper's wife. She likes to prepare delicious meals for her husband.*

● Model the first example to ensure everybody understands the task.

● Share the learning objectives with the class, according to the specific evidence you wish to collect and set success criteria for each differentiated group.

● Use the writing to make judgements against specific assessment focuses.

Assessment

It happened like this...

● Write one sentence to describe who is in each picture. Then write about their role in the story.

Illustration © 1977, David Armitage.

SCHOLASTIC
www.scholastic.co.uk

READ & RESPOND: Activities based on The Lighthouse Keeper's Lunch